THIS BOOK BELONGS TO:

Let's get started...

LOVED THE PAGES? LEAVE A NOTE!

Hey there! I'm David, a globe-trotter turned devoted dad of three, crafting these coloring adventures from Hamburg. Your reviews are vital, helping me inspire more young minds across the globe. Just a minute of your time to share your thoughts would mean the world to me. Every review, yours especially, is cherished. Thank you for your support and happy coloring!

Sincerely,
David Christiansen

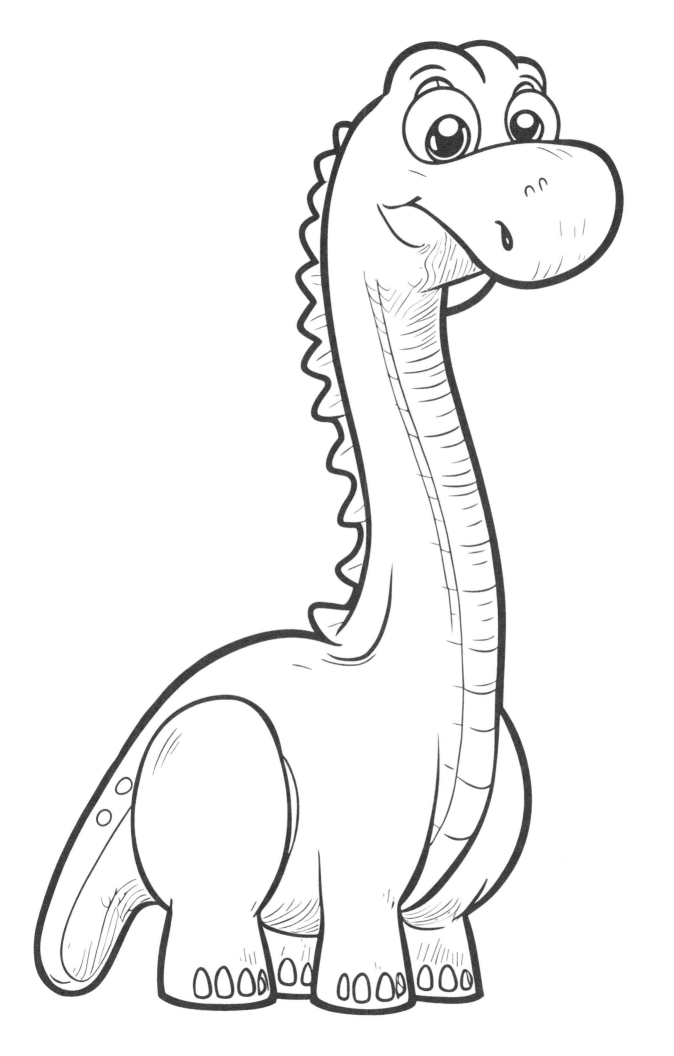

Dear Young Artists & Families,

Thank you for bringing color and life to the pages of this book. Each stroke of your crayon or pencil adds magic to these illustrations, creating a world of vibrant colors and joyful memories. As the creator of this book, my greatest reward is seeing your imagination at play.

Your thoughts and experiences matter greatly to me. If you've enjoyed our colorful journey, I invite you to share your feedback in an Amazon review. Your words not only brighten my day but also guide me in crafting more delightful adventures for you. Feel free to reach out with your creative ideas, suggestions, or just a hello at info@warmoakstudios.com. And if you're curious about our future artistic voyages, updates are always waiting for you at news@warmoakstudios.com.

Every review and message is a treasure, contributing to the growth of this book and my journey as an author. Your voices inspire and encourage me, and for that, I am profoundly grateful.

With heartfelt thanks and colorful wishes,
David Christiansen, Warm Oak Studios

LIKE THIS BOOK?
RE-ORDER AS GIFT:

https://mybook.to/toddlerdinosaur

 info@warmoakstudios.com

 news@warmoakstudios.com

 https://warmoakstudios.com

WARM OAK
Studios